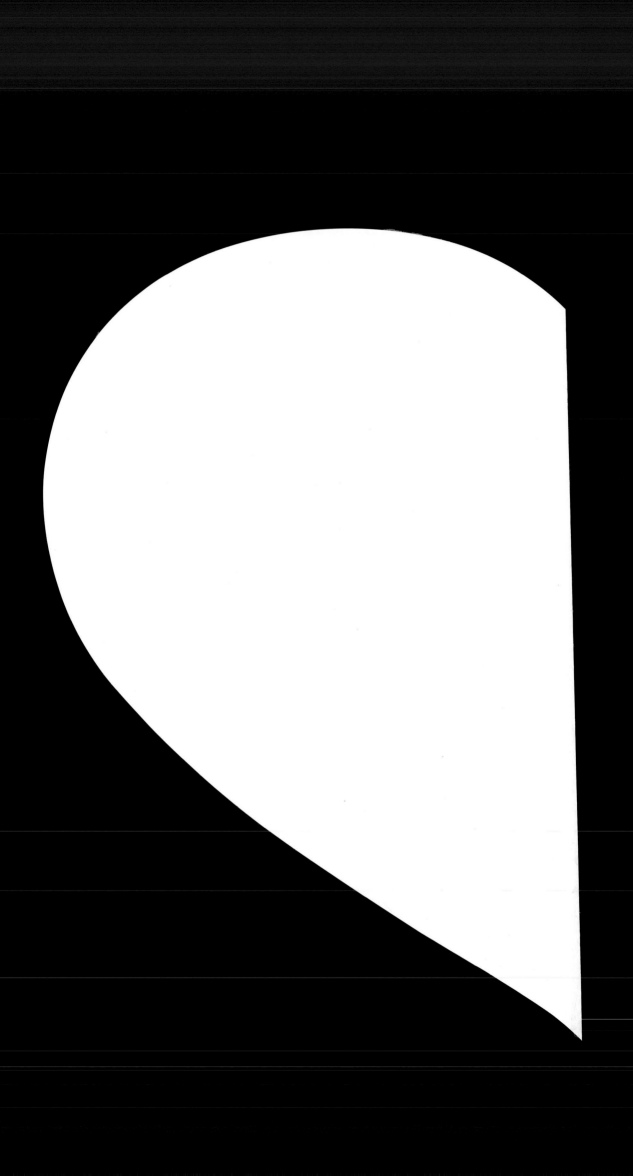

LOVE SIGNS

LORI REID

♈ ♉ ♊ ♋ ♌ ♍

LOVE SIGNS

♎ ♏ ♐ ♑ ♒ ♓

DUNCAN BAIRD PUBLISHERS
LONDON

For Elouise Rowe: may you find love wherever you go

Love Signs
Lori Reid

Distributed in the USA and Canada by Sterling Publishing Co., Inc.
387 Park Avenue South, New York, NY 10016-8810

This edition first published in the UK and USA in 2007 by
Duncan Baird Publishers Ltd, Sixth Floor, Castle House,
75–76 Wells Street, London W1T 3QH

Managing Designer: Manisha Patel
Designer: Luana Gobbo
Managing Editor: Grace Cheetham
Editor: Ingrid Court-Jones
Commissioned artwork: Flatliner V2

Library of Congress Cataloging-in-Publication Data Available
ISBN-13: 978-1-84483-325-2
ISBN-10: 1-84483-325-9
10 9 8 7 6 5 4 3 2 1

Typeset in Optima
Color reproduction by Colourscan, Singapore
Printed in China by Imago

For information about custom editions, special sales,
premium and corporate purchases, please contact
Sterling Special Sales Department at 800-805-5489
or specialsales@sterlingpub.com.

Contents

6 LOVE & THE ZODIAC

8 Cosmic Love
10 Finding Your Sun Sign
12 Earth, Air, Fire, & Water
14 Finding Your Moon Sign
16 Moon Chart 1
18 Moon Chart 2
19 Moon Chart 3

20 THE TWELVE LOVE SIGNS

22 ♈ Aries
30 ♉ Taurus
38 ♊ Gemini
46 ♋ Cancer
54 ♌ Leo
62 ♍ Virgo
70 ♎ Libra
78 ♏ Scorpio
86 ♐ Sagittarius
94 ♑ Capricorn
102 ♒ Aquarius
110 ♓ Pisces

118 WHEN TO MEET & WHEN TO MOVE ON

120 Time for Living & Loving
122 Hot Dates
126 Moving On

128 Acknowledgments

Are **you** ready to open your heart to **love**?
If so, read on …

cosmic love

It's quite likely that you know your star sign, but do you know which element you belong to, or which sign the moon was in on the day you were born? It's this kind of information that gives you a deeper understanding of your emotions, of who you are, what makes you tick, who is on your wavelength, and, more important, whom you're destined to fall in love with.

Using this book
First off, there's information on the twelve signs of the Zodiac (also known as sun signs) on pages 10–11, and you'll be able to find your own sign and see how it fits into the scheme of things. On pages 12–13 you can discover your element—whether you're an earth, air, fire, or water type. Believe it or not, your element type has a fundamental effect on your character and shows the kind of people you're drawn to.

Then comes your moon sign. You won't find anything about this when you read your horoscope in a newspaper or a magazine, and yet your moon sign gives you so much information on your emotions, what affects you deeply, what you like and dislike, how you respond to people, and, crucially, what kind of a lover you are. The more you know about your moon sign, the more you'll understand about your feelings, your deepest desires, your innermost loves and hates. It's your moon sign that tells you about your moods and reactions, how you get on with others, and the kinds of relationship you're likely to have.

Finding your moon sign is a little involved, but we've made it easy and fun for you to do. You'll find all the instructions you need on pages 15–19.

So, are you a gutsy Aries, a girlie Libra, or a streetwise Scorpio? Whatever your star sign, there's a lot more to discover about yourself—and your love life—in the Twelve Love Signs section. You'll find eight whole pages devoted just to you. Check it out.

And finally, it's back to the moon again. Did you know that the moon affects you on a day-to-day basis? It can influence your mood: how excited or calm, lively or lazy you're feeling, and what you feel like doing. What you enjoy, whom you like to be with, and where you like to go are subtly determined by the phase the moon is in. The section When To Meet & When To Move On, on pages 118–127, will give you all the lowdown—so go on, give it a try!

finding your sun sign

Although you're a unique and special person, you have characteristics that you share in common with the other people who were born at the same time as you, and who therefore belong to the same sun sign.

There are twelve sun signs, which start with Aries and end with Pisces. Each covers a period of about a month and is associated with certain personality traits. For example, if you're a Gemini, you're bubbly and witty, whereas if you're Cancerian, you're much quieter and tend to hide inside your shell.

Ingeniously, the ancients gave each sun sign a symbol, which encapsulates its qualities and characteristics. For example, Aries is a ram—a fast and feisty creature, which sums up people born under that sign.

Each sign is also depicted by a "glyph," a kind of shorthand picture. Take Taurus. Here, you see the head of a bull—the animal that represents the sign. Or Sagittarius. Its glyph is a depiction of part of its symbol—the Centaur's arrow.

To find your sun sign, simply look at the dates on the outer ring of the chart opposite, and see which sector your birthday falls in. This gives you the name of your sun sign and also shows its glyph.

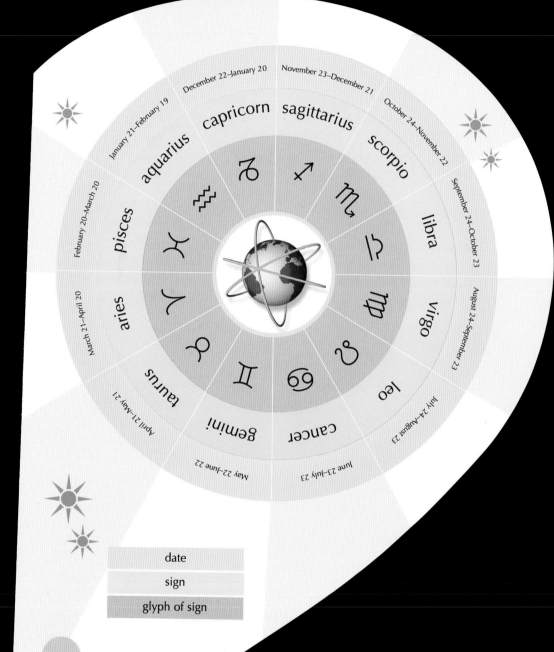

December 22–January 20 November 23–December 21

January 21–February 19 capricorn sagittarius October 24–November 22

aquarius scorpio

February 20–March 20 pisces libra September 24–October 23

aries virgo August 24–September 23

March 21–April 20

taurus leo July 24–August 23

April 21–May 21

gemini cancer

May 22–June 22 June 23–July 23

date

sign

glyph of sign

11

earth, air, fire & water

The element your sign belongs to gives further clues as to how you go about things. There are four element groups—earth, air, fire, and water—each containing three signs. Your element endows you with certain qualities, which you share with the other members of the three signs in your group. This gives you a common bond with your fellow element members, so that you're more in tune, or on the same wavelength as each other.

EARTH
Signs: ♉, ♍, ♑
Element influence: You're practical, hardworking, busy, reliable, and full of common sense.

AIR
Signs: ♊, ♎, ♒
Element influence: You're bright, sociable, chatty, stimulating, restless, and full of ideas.

FIRE
Signs: ♈, ♌, ♐
Element influence: You're warm, active, dynamic, enthusiastic, and full of life and energy.

WATER
Signs: ♋, ♏, ♓
Element influence: You're sensitive, emotional, caring, intuitive, and full of imagination.

Element compatibility

Throughout life you'll discover that you're naturally drawn to people who share your element because you understand each other and tend to experience things in a similar kind of way. But how do you get along with the people in the other element groups? Do you make fertile soil together (earth + water), creative steam (fire + water), pretty bubbles (air + water)? Or do you blow up a sandstorm (earth + air) and explode like a volcano (earth + fire)? You see how it works! Now, match your element with the others to find out how well you get along.

	EARTH ♉ ♍ ♑	AIR ♊ ♎ ♒	FIRE ♈ ♌ ♐	WATER ♋ ♏ ♓
W A T E R	Supportive and refreshing, you're comfortable and well-suited together.	Sometimes stormy, sometimes fun. You need to get the balance right here.	Could be powerful, but you're emotionally different, so this match will be a challenge.	A sensitive and devoted pair able to understand and empathize with each other's highs and lows.
F I R E	You're very different people with different needs, moods, and responses, so it won't be easy.	You're both amusing, lively, and fun so you have plenty here to keep each other happy.	Masses of enthusiasm, energy, and warmth make you an exciting and dynamic duo.	
A I R	With conflicting needs, feelings, and ideas, you need to meet in the middle for this to work.	You're flexible, think alike, and are always on the move together; you're an ideal twosome.		
E A R T H	Ambitious, hard-working, solid, and organized, you know where you're going and you're both on the same road.			

finding your moon sign

Believe it or not, the moon affects our moods! It may be subtle, but the moon's influence is pretty powerful. After all, it's the moon that creates the tides, pulling and pushing great oceans from one side of our planet to the other. Now, because we human beings are made up mostly of water, this great magnetic pull must surely work on our brains and bodies, too.

You've heard how people behave oddly at the time of the full moon. For centuries, myths and stories have associated the full moon with werewolves, ghosts, and strange happenings. That may be far-fetched, but research has shown that people do behave erratically, get overexcited, and have more arguments and illnesses at this time of the month than at any other.

But it's not just at full moon that we're affected—it's throughout the month as the moon moves through its four phases: from new moon to first quarter to full moon and last quarter, before disappearing altogether. Then it reappears as a shiny new crescent to start the cycle all over again. These four phases each last for about a week, the whole cycle taking a month to complete. Incidentally, the word "month," or "moonth," as it used to be called, simply means a "four-week moon period."

The moon's energies change with each phase, and it's this changing energy that we subconsciously pick up and tune in to through the month. For example, when the moon's energies are weak. Strength and just before a new moon, when the moon's energies are weak. Strength and vitality build as the moon waxes during the first quarter, and many people get quite charged up on the days around the full moon, only to quieten down again as the moon wanes.

As well as its four phases, the moon also moves through the twelve signs of the Zodiac each month, spending about two-and-a-quarter days in each sign. This is important because astrologically the moon rules our feelings and emotions. How you react to people, how you respond to situations, what affects you deeply, what makes you happy, sad, or wanting to sing for joy—all depend on the sign the moon was in on the day you were born.

Calculating your moon sign

In the next few pages you'll find easy-to-follow instructions about how to calculate your moon sign using the specially devised Moon Charts. Discovering your moon sign will give you another insight into what makes you unique and so special—so what are you waiting for? Turn to page 16 now!

Moon Chart 1

Run your finger down the column until you find the year in which you were born. Then move your finger across to the month of your birth. Make a mental note of the symbol given and turn to page 18.

YEAR OF BIRTH		JAN	FEB	MAR	APR	MAY
1977	1996	♉	♋	♋	♍	♎
1978	1997	♎	♏	♐	♑	♒
1979	1998	♒	♈	♈	♊	♋
1980	1999	♊	♌	♌	♎	♏
1981	2000	♏	♐	♑	♒	♈
1982	2001	♓	♉	♉	♋	♌
1983	2002	♌	♍	♎	♏	♐
1984	2003	♐	♊	♊	♌	♍
1985	2004	♈	♊	♊	♑	♒
1986	2005	♍	♏	♏	♉	♊
1987	2006	♑	♓	♓	♍	♎
1988	2007	♉	♋	♋	♍	♓
1989	2008	♎	♐	♐	♒	♓
1990	2009	♓	♈	♉	♊	♋
1991	2010	♋	♍	♍	♎	♐
1992	2011	♏	♑	♑	♓	♈
1993	2012	♈	♉	♊	♌	♍
1994	2013	♌	♎	♎	♐	♑
1995	2014	♑	♒	♓	♈	♉

JUN	JUL	AUG	SEP	OCT	NOV	DEC
♐	♑	♒	♈	♉	♋	♌
♈	♉	♋	♌	♍	♏	♐
♌	♍	♏	♑	♒	♈	♉
♑	♒	♈	♉	♊	♌	♍
♉	♊	♌	♎	♏	♐	♑
♎	♏	♐	♒	♓	♉	♊
♒	♓	♉	♋	♌	♍	♎
♊	♌	♍	♏	♐	♒	♓
♏	♐	♒	♓	♈	♊	♋
♓	♉	♊	♌	♍	♎	♐
♌	♍	♏	♐	♑	♓	♈
♐	♑	♓	♈	♊	♋	♌
♉	♊	♋	♍	♎	♐	♑
♍	♎	♐	♑	♒	♈	♉
♑	♓	♈	♊	♋	♍	♉
♊	♋	♍	♏	♐	♑	♎
♎	♏	♑	♓	♈	♉	♋
♓	♈	♉	♋	♌	♎	♏
♋	♌	♎	♏	♑	♒	♈

THE TWELVE LOVE SIGNS

♈ Aries
♉ Taurus
♊ Gemini
♋ Cancer
♌ Leo
♍ Virgo
♎ Libra
♏ Scorpio
♐ Sagittarius
♑ Capricorn
♒ Aquarius
♓ Pisces

17

Moon Chart 2

YOU WERE BORN ON THIS DAY:	ADD THIS MANY SIGNS:	YOU WERE BORN ON THIS DAY:	ADD THIS MANY SIGNS:
1	0	16	7
2	1	17	7
3	1	18	8
4	1	19	8
5	2	20	9
6	2	21	9
7	3	22	10
8	3	23	10
9	4	24	10
10	4	25	11
11	5	26	11
12	5	27	12
13	5	28	12
14	6	29	1
15	6	30	1
		31	2

Look at Moon Chart 2, above. Find the day of the month on which you were born. The number to the right of that day tells you how many extra Zodiac signs you need to add on from the sign you were allocated in Moon Chart 1.

Moon Chart 3

Moon Chart 3 shows the Zodiac with the twelve signs. Put your finger on the sign you were shown in Moon Chart 1. Then, moving clockwise, count on the extra number of signs indicated in Moon Chart 2. The sign you arrive at is the sign the moon was in on the day you were born.

Whatever sign you belong to, **love** is a potent, passionate, exciting, and empowering **emotion.**

the twelve love signs

Courageous

Impulsive

Daring

Active

Inventive

First

Fast

22

Ɣ Aries

Dates: March 21–April 20

Ruling Planet: Mars

Element: Fire

Color: Scarlet

Flowers: Red rose, honeysuckle

Precious Stone: Diamond

♈ Aries

about you

You're always in a hurry, Aries. If you're not running, or playing physical sports, you're rushing to get from A to B. Partly, it's because you're impatient. But mainly it's because belonging to the first sign of the Zodiac means you're pre-programmed to get in front of everyone else and take the lead.

Winning is very important to you. You're hugely competitive and a born champion. That's why you excel at games: running, field sports, martial arts, or any activity where you can beat your opponent with speed and skill.

It's that same drive to be first that draws you to become an explorer, inventor, or pioneer. You're fascinated by the latest technology. Where you're concerned, any new gadget on the market is simply a must-have.

In appearance, you probably have high cheekbones and thick or wavy hair. Your love of the outdoors adds a healthy glow to your complexion. Emotionally, you're romantic—but you're not afraid to make the first move.

In your haste to win, watch out that you don't push others aside! You wouldn't like to be construed as selfish, now, would you?

Most lovable quality: Your enthusiasm

Biggest need: To WIN!

Favorite way to chill out: Mixing music

You adore: Sports

You dislike: People who push in front of you

Wicked pleasure: Bagging the best bargain in the sales

Fashion style: Anything sporty, comfortable, easy to wear, and— within close reach

Best for your looks: Hats, hoods, baseball caps

You'd win a gold medal in the Olympics if they gave an award for: Selfishness

Well-being workout: Cross-country running

heart & soul

You're a bright spark, a real go-getter, and someone who always likes to be at the forefront of the action. But does your moon sign spur you on to better things or hold you back? Read on to find out.

Incidentally, if you don't know your moon sign already, you can find instructions on how to calculate it on pages 15–19.

◐ in Aries

Strong and robust, you're no crybaby, are you? In relationships, you like to be the boss.

◐ in Taurus

Will you go for adventure or security? You're gutsy enough to go for both—but you must get the balance right.

◐ in Gemini

Your attention span is very short and limited, which means that emotionally you get bored very quickly.

◐ in Cancer

Much as you try to hide that soft center, your sensitivity keeps peeping through. Let it! You're a nicer person because of it.

◐ in Leo

You're certainly a fast mover. And you're very confident and sure of yourself—which is great!

26

☽ in Virgo

You think of the consequences before you take that mighty leap, which makes you a good deal more sensible than most other Aries.

☽ in Libra

This moon placement smoothes out all your rough edges and makes you a highly desirable chick.

☽ in Scorpio

Yikes! You're one strong lady with tremendous depth and power. You will win, come hell or high water.

☽ in Sagittarius

Hot or what, Aries? Life's a gas for you as you reach farther, faster, and higher than anyone else.

☽ in Capricorn

You know where you're going, and, with your determination and ambition, nothing and no one will stop you from getting there!

☽ in Aquarius

Friendly and sociable you may be, but ultimately you like to do your own thing in your own way.

☽ in Pisces

You're romantic, and because you're more considerate than most Aries, you're a prize catch!

compatibility

You may be a competitive Aries, but you're also sentimental, and you fall in and out of love with breathtaking speed. It's the chase that excites you, the challenge of capturing the heart of that special someone. But what is your ideal mate like? Well, he needs to be someone strong and active, a guy who knows his own mind, who's independent and full of fun, and who keeps you guessing. So who turns your head, sends goose bumps up your arms, and drives you wild with longing? Most likely another fire sign—Leo or Sagittarius, perhaps. Members of the earth and water signs are probably less compatible—they may be too slow, too sensitive, or too stuck in their ways for your robust and impulsive nature. However, Gemini and Aquarius, who are both air signs, could prove a great match. Take a look at the Celestial Combinations, opposite—you can use either your sun or moon sign to find your true affinity.

LOVE HEART RATINGS

perilous = ❤

problematical = ❤❤

possible = ❤❤❤

promising = ❤❤❤❤

perfect = ❤❤❤❤❤

28

Celestial Combinations

YOUR SUN OR MOON SIGN WITH:

Aries   Hot, hasty, and competitive, but great mates.   ❤❤❤❤

Taurus   Tantalizing, but you each want different things.   ❤❤

Gemini   Plenty here to keep you amused.   ❤❤❤❤

Cancer   Okay if you can stay sensitive to each other's needs.   ❤❤

Leo   Passionate and fiery, you're well matched.   ❤❤❤❤

Virgo   Will work only if you can reconcile your differing views.   ❤

Libra   Conflicting needs, but you can learn a lot from each other.

❤❤❤

Scorpio   Masses of competition here to drive you on.   ❤❤❤

Sagittarius   Loads of love, energy, and plans.   ❤❤❤❤

Capricorn   You'll need patience if you want this to work.

❤❤❤

Aquarius   A sparkling pair—you keep each other
well entertained.   ❤❤❤❤

Pisces   You admire each other
from afar.   ❤❤

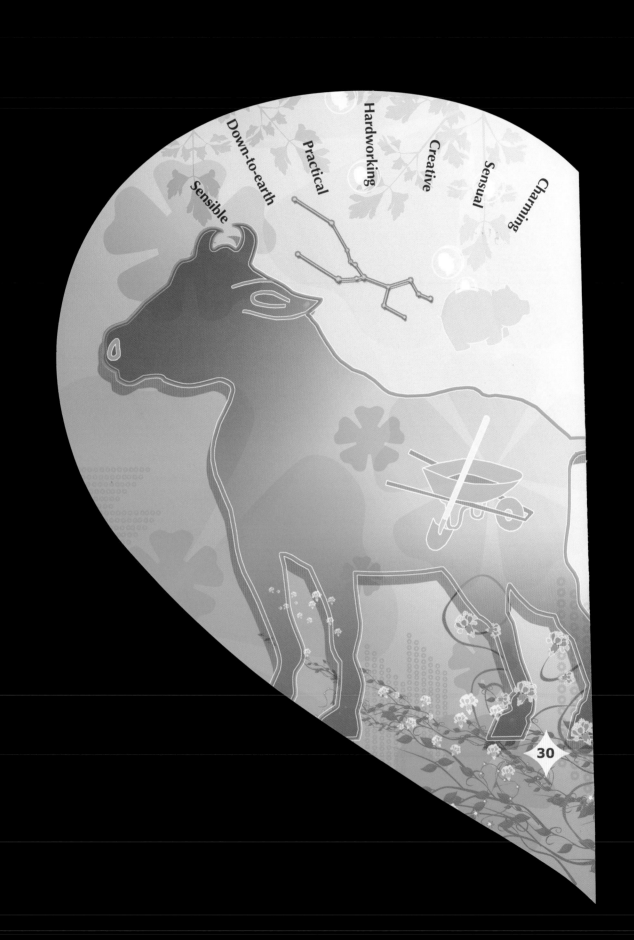

Charming

Sensual

Creative

Hardworking

Practical

Down-to-earth

Sensible

30

♉ Taurus

Dates: April 21–May 21

Ruling Planet: Venus

Element: Earth

Colors: Green, light blue, pink

Flowers: Carnation, violet

Precious Stone: Emerald

♉ Taurus

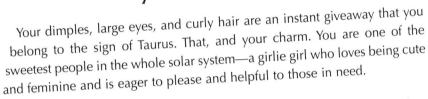

about you

Your dimples, large eyes, and curly hair are an instant giveaway that you belong to the sign of Taurus. That, and your charm. You are one of the sweetest people in the whole solar system—a girlie girl who loves being cute and feminine and is eager to please and helpful to those in need.

Taureans are described as sensual—and it's true! Above all, you adore comfort: plenty of food, drink, and money to ensure you're well cushioned. What helps you sleep well at night is knowing you're safe, secure, and cozy.

But that doesn't mean you're a pushover. You may be indulgent, but you're also a hard worker. In fact, underneath all the sugar lies a tough cookie. Solid and sensible, you'll hang in there until you get what you want.

Your tenacity stands you in good stead. But its flip side—stubbornness—means that sometimes you don't know when to let go.

Ruled by Venus, you have a very loving nature, and when you fall in love you're a loyal partner, committing yourself body and soul. But beware of jealousy and possessiveness, which can work against you in close relationships.

Most lovable quality: Charm

Biggest need: Creature comforts

Favorite way to chill out: Reading magazines

You adore: Being spoiled and pampered

You hate: Anyone taking your stuff

Wicked pleasure: French pastries

Fashion style: Feminine but comfortable

Best for your looks: Necklaces, scarves, collars, and chokers

You'd win a gold medal in the Olympics if they gave an award for: Shopping

Well-being workout: Dancing

heart & soul

You like to plod along in your own sweet way, don't you, Taurus? But if you're not typical of your sun sign, perhaps it's your moon placement that gives you a turbo charge. Read on to find out.

If you don't know your moon sign already, you can find instructions on how to calculate it on pages 15–19.

◐ in Aries

You have a good deal more get-up-and-go than the average Taurean. In relationships, you like to make the first move.

◐ in Taurus

Solid but a touch stolid—you know how to get your own way, and you'll hang on in there until you do!

◐ in Gemini

Not just a pretty face—you're clever and know how to use your charm to best effect. You'll go far!

◐ in Cancer

Hardworking, steadfast, loyal, and true. You're an asset to your family and the best friend anyone could want.

◐ in Leo

What a luxury-loving person you are, Taurus. It has to be five-star living all the way for you, and nothing less.

◑ in Virgo

You're so earthy, so logical, so practical. But details matter, so things—and people—have to be just right.

◑ in Libra

You're so creative, so talented, so musical—but you have difficulty deciding which road to follow.

◑ in Scorpio

Focused and intense, you've got what it takes to become a millionaire!

◑ in Sagittarius

You're not as inflexible as a lot of other Taureans. This moon makes you more easygoing and a lot luckier, too.

◑ in Capricorn

Strong, solid, and sound, you're a great organizer who's destined to go far.

◑ in Aquarius

You not only have a great imagination, but you're practical, too. That could make you a really successful inventor.

◑ in Pisces

Come on, loosen up, Taurus! If you listen to that inner voice more often and follow your intuition, you won't go far wrong.

Taurus

compatibility

Taureans don't rush love. They go for the slow burn, taking their time before handing over the keys to their hearts. As one of these, you know yourself how you adore the early stages of a romance: the flirting, the shy smiles, that funny flutter your heart makes when his name lights up your cellphone screen. What you're looking for in a soul mate is someone you can trust—a guy who is dependable, solid, and down-to-earth and who knows how to make you feel special. You're in perfect synch with other members of the earth fraternity—Virgo, Capricorn, and, of course, Taurus. You should also get along very well with anyone belonging to the water trio. However, fire and air could prove trickier, either because they come on too strong for you or because you find them unreliable. But check out the Celestial Combinations, opposite. Match either your sun or moon sign to find your perfect pairing.

LOVE HEART RATINGS

perilous = ♥

problematical = ♥♥

possible = ♥♥♥

promising = ♥♥♥♥

perfect = ♥♥♥♥♥

♥ 36

Celestial Combinations

YOUR SUN OR MOON SIGN WITH:

Aries	Your priorities differ in lots of ways.	♥♥
Taurus	You're both bossy but love each other to pieces.	♥♥♥♥
Gemini	Differing attitudes divide you.	♥
Cancer	You complement each other so much.	♥♥♥♥
Leo	Talk about having fun! This lion will spoil you silly.	♥♥♥
Virgo	As solid as a rock!	♥♥♥♥♥
Libra	Music, dance, and art are shared passions.	♥♥♥
Scorpio	You're both strong and stubborn—but that's the challenge.	♥♥♥
Sagittarius	You'll have to compromise to avoid a clash.	♥
Capricorn	A powerful relationship destined for great things.	♥♥♥♥♥
Aquarius	You'll need lots of trust to make this work.	♥♥
Pisces	Mutually supportive and tender—lovely!	♥♥♥

Vivacious

Dextrous

Articulate

Quick

Clever

Chatty

Sociable

♊ Gemini

Dates: May 22–June 22

Ruling Planet: Mercury

Element: Air

Color: Yellow

Flowers: Honeysuckle, lily of the valley

Precious Stone: Agate

♊ Gemini

about you

You can always tell a Gemini by their bright, alert eyes. They may be having a one-to-one conversation with you, but they won't miss a thing going on in the room. And they can't sit still—they fidget, shuffle their feet, and drum their fingers. Oh yes, and they're never lost for words!

You can't help loving a Gemini, because they're so bubbly and effervescent. Belonging to this sign makes you sparkling and witty, great company and amusing to have around.

Your restless, inquiring mind makes you insatiably curious. Clever and quick to learn, you have the ability to size up a situation in the twinkling of an eye. You get bored really quickly, so you need a lot of variety—heaps of different interests and friends.

You're especially skilled at languages and probably spend more time on the phone than all the other star signs put together! And you're doubly quick with replies to flirty lines.

You like to have lots of admirers, but only those who can keep you amused, interested, and intrigued will find a way into your heart.

40

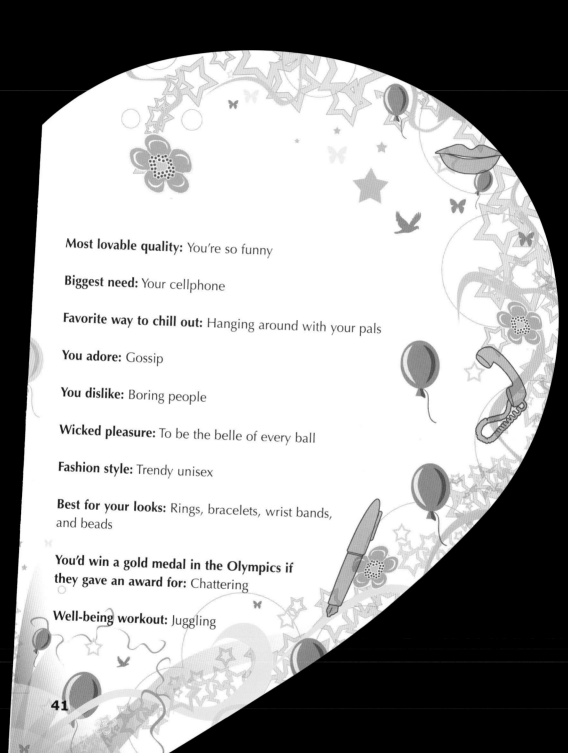

Most lovable quality: You're so funny

Biggest need: Your cellphone

Favorite way to chill out: Hanging around with your pals

You adore: Gossip

You dislike: Boring people

Wicked pleasure: To be the belle of every ball

Fashion style: Trendy unisex

Best for your looks: Rings, bracelets, wrist bands, and beads

You'd win a gold medal in the Olympics if they gave an award for: Chattering

Well-being workout: Juggling

41

heart & soul

You're quite a live wire, aren't you, Gemini? But then you knew that already. Perhaps what you didn't know is that your moon sign can give your character a subtle twist. Want to know more? Then read on.

If you don't know your moon sign already, you can find instructions on how to calculate it on pages 15–19.

☽ in Aries
Mentally and emotionally dynamic, you like to mix with people; and, be honest, you can be a huge flirt, can't you?

☽ in Taurus
This moon gives you a good deal more staying power and the ability to turn your ingenious ideas into practical reality.

☽ in Gemini
You're highly gifted and clever, both intellectually and creatively. You're a real shining star.

☽ in Cancer
With a memory like yours, you could be a champion at quizzes and could make your fortune in the process.

☽ in Leo
Acting, singing, dancing—you choose. You're a born showbiz girl, destined for the limelight one way or another.

◑ in Virgo

Chatter, chatter, chatter. You're so silver-tongued, Gemini, and so technically accomplished. Time to stop talking and get doing.

◑ in Libra

You're blessed with the gift of the gab, Gemini. With all that charm and potential you could sell snow to Alaska.

◑ in Scorpio

There's no sharper eye, no more penetrating mind, and no deeper intuition than yours.

◑ in Sagittarius

You're a seeker after knowledge. Travel will figure highly throughout your life and career.

◑ in Capricorn

You're good at languages, IT, art, and science. If you combine them all, you'll make a fortune.

◑ in Aquarius

With talents as good as yours, the world is your oyster. You should think very big.

◑ in Pisces

Whether it's plays, musical scores, or computer programs, the upshot is the same—you're a born writer.

Gemini

compatibility

Looks aren't necessarily the first thing that draw you to a guy. What attracts you is personality, wit, intelligence, and a genius for keeping you amused. Don't forget about that low boredom threshold of yours, which means that you can tire of people at the click of your fingers. It's said that Gemini likes to play the field. Well, yes, it's true—you do—but only because you're looking for that perfect person who has the knack of keeping you interested and amused. So who will tickle your ribs and bring a smile to your face? The fire signs and people from your own air group are a good bet. For example, Geminis and Aquarians make a great team. And so do Geminis and Leos. Earth and water, though, can bog you down a bit. But check out the Celestial Combinations, opposite, for a clearer definition. Don't forget, you can match either your sun or your moon sign to find the ideal heartthrob for you.

LOVE HEART RATINGS

perilous = ❤
problematical = ❤❤
possible = ❤❤❤
promising = ❤❤❤❤
perfect = ❤❤❤❤❤

Celestial Combinations

YOUR SUN OR MOON SIGN WITH:

Aries	Wow! What a high-octane romance!	❤❤❤❤
Taurus	You're on different planes—can you meet in the middle?	❤
Gemini	Inventive, witty, and a laugh a minute!	❤❤❤❤
Cancer	Socially, you like different things.	❤❤
Leo	Plenty of sparks keep your relationship bright.	❤❤❤❤
Virgo	This partner provides an anchor if you need it.	❤❤❤
Libra	One of the best combinations in the Zodiac!	❤❤❤❤❤
Scorpio	Little meeting of minds makes this a long shot.	❤
Sagittarius	You're opposites, but together you can sparkle.	❤❤❤
Capricorn	This partner will keep your feet on the ground.	❤
Aquarius	You fit together like two pieces of a jigsaw.	❤❤❤❤❤
Pisces	Only with plenty of give-and-take.	❤❤

Sensitive

Home-loving

Intuitive

Emotional

Family-oriented

Protective

Nurturing

46

Dates: June 23–July 23

Ruling Planet: Moon

Element: Water

Color: Silver

Flower: Water lily

Precious Stones: Pearl, moonstone

Cancer

69 Cancer

about you

Fair skin and a round face characterize the typical Cancerian. You're blessed with expressive eyes and a devastating film-star smile that takes people's breath away.

Your ruler, the moon, is a strong influence in your life. For a start, you're a nurturing person, protective of those you love. You are also one of the most sensitive signs. Intuitive and imaginative, warm and caring—your family and your home are the center of your universe. In fact, you're never happier than when you're puttering around the house. Cancerians are especially close to their mothers—a bond that is likely to stay with them for life.

You love history, as you're drawn to the past. You enjoy amassing objects and artifacts that you believe will one day make your fortune. And your memory is one of the best in the Zodiac!

Emotionally, you're very tender and get hurt easily. If someone or something upsets you, like your symbol, the crab, you retreat quite smartly into your shell.

Although your moods fluctuate like the tides, you are at heart a true romantic.

Most lovable quality: Your kindness

Biggest need: To know that your family is there for you

Favorite way to chill out: Sorting through your collections

You adore: Your mom

You dislike: Anyone who says anything horrible about your mom (or other members of your family)

Wicked pleasure: Wallowing in a bubbly spa bath

Fashion style: Soft and feminine

Best for your looks: Badges, pins, brooches, silvery or pearly pendants

You'd win a gold medal in the Olympics if they gave an award for: Worrying

Well-being workout: Aqua-aerobics

heart & soul

It's true that all Cancerians love their roots, their family, and their homes. But there's more to you than little Miss Apple Pie—as your moon sign will show. Read on to find out more.

If you don't know your moon sign already, you can find instructions on how to calculate it on pages 15–19.

◐ in Aries
A good-news moon that makes you emotionally tougher than other Cancerians, and not so moody, either.

◐ in Taurus
You're a great judge of character, Cancer. It's an unerring talent that will take you far.

◐ in Gemini
You're a clever crab and not as moody as other members of your sign.

◐ in Cancer
You're soft, tender, and oh so sensitive. As long as you have a loving family around you, you'll be okay.

◐ in Leo
You have a brilliant knack for making money, which is just as well, as you like to have nice things.

☽ in Virgo
You're a caring, sharing person, Cancer, and your talents could well lead to a career in the medical profession.

☽ in Libra
You have a good blend of energies which produces a charming, gracious, and elegant personality.

☽ in Scorpio
As you're such a tender Crab, your protective shell is probably your best friend.

☽ in Sagittarius
Great! This moon means you won't take yourself quite so seriously, Cancer, which has to be good news for you.

☽ in Capricorn
Because this moon always adds an old head on young shoulders, it means you're emotionally mature.

☽ in Aquarius
Is your head ruling your heart, or your heart ruling your head? Whichever, it's not a bad combination at all.

☽ in Pisces
That nurturing instinct of yours makes you one of life's givers, and the world is a richer place for that.

compatibility

All Cancerians thrive on love. They also need to feel safe and secure. That's what you're looking for in a relationship: someone who will cherish and protect you, who will take you in their arms and shield you from the harsher realities of life. So where will you find this gorgeous hunk? Probably among the members of the earth element—Taurus, Virgo, and Capricorn. Not only will they understand you, but they'll also give you that essential sense of security that you need to help to ground you. And if you're looking for someone to float your boat, you need look no further than the water signs, Scorpio and Pisces, as well as other Cancerians, of course. However, fire and air signs tend to unsettle you. You find the first group too fiery and the second far too breezy for comfort. But take a look at the Celestial Combinations, opposite. Finding a match either to your sun or moon sign will reveal the sweetheart of your dreams.

LOVE HEART RATINGS

perilous = ❤

problematical = ❤❤

possible = ❤❤❤

promising = ❤❤❤❤

perfect = ❤❤❤❤❤

Celestial Combinations

YOUR SUN OR MOON SIGN WITH:

Aries A little outside your comfort zone, but could be fun. ❤

Taurus Wonderful—you both adore your creature comforts.
❤❤❤❤

Gemini Laughter, yes. Permanency? Probably not. ❤

Cancer Caring, sharing, and deeply loving. ❤❤❤❤❤

Leo Fine, if you're happy to let this partner take charge. ❤❤❤

Virgo You're a winning team in every way. ❤❤❤❤

Libra You're attracted, but will it last? ❤

Scorpio A powerful chemistry draws you together. ❤❤❤❤❤

Sagittarius Good to begin with, but difficult to sustain. ❤❤

Capricorn Although you're opposites, there's lots of caring here.
❤❤❤

Aquarius Plenty of compromise is the only way. ❤❤

Pisces This is heavenly—you're so good for
each other. ❤❤❤❤❤

Aristocratic

Vital

Generous

Loving

Leader/hero

Dynamic

Extrovert

♌ Leo

Dates: July 24–August 23

Ruling Planet: Sun

Element: Fire

Colors: Gold, orange

Flowers: Sunflower, marigold

Precious Stone: Ruby

Leo

about you

Just like the lion, the king of the jungle, who symbolically rules your sign, you have a wonderful mane of hair and you carry yourself with regal bearing. Courageous and magnetic, you're warm and attractive.

There are lots of similarities between Leos and cats. Sometimes you can be cute and cuddly like a fluffy kitten. At other times you can be fierce and temperamental, and you roar with rage. You can be a party animal, but you also like to curl up quietly in front of the fire.

There's no doubt your dramatic qualities get you noticed. From a young age you learn to perform and to be applauded. You enjoy being in the spotlight, so it's no surprise that Leos make great actors.

As well as being a talented performer, you're very artistic and creative. A good organizer, you like to take charge. You're a loyal and honest friend, but watch out for that bossy streak!

In relationships you're romantic and lovable. When you set your sights on someone, you revert to your leonine nature, moving stealthily and purposely until you catch your "prey."

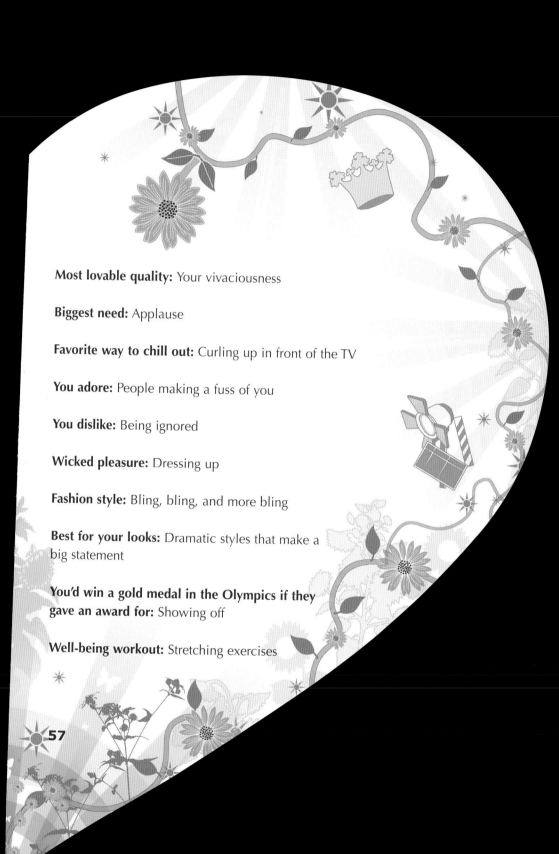

Most lovable quality: Your vivaciousness

Biggest need: Applause

Favorite way to chill out: Curling up in front of the TV

You adore: People making a fuss of you

You dislike: Being ignored

Wicked pleasure: Dressing up

Fashion style: Bling, bling, and more bling

Best for your looks: Dramatic styles that make a big statement

You'd win a gold medal in the Olympics if they gave an award for: Showing off

Well-being workout: Stretching exercises

Leo

heart & soul

Bright, dramatic, vivacious, full of life. Yes, you're all those things, but you're a whole heap more besides. And what makes the big difference is your moon sign. Check it out here.

If you don't know your moon sign already, you can find instructions on how to calculate it on pages 15–19.

☽ in Aries

You're a powerful person who likes to be in charge and in control. You may be bold and brave, but you're oh so romantic, too.

☽ in Taurus

This moon gives you staying power and the ability to work hard so you can afford all the luxuries you desire.

☽ in Gemini

This is a really frothy combination that makes you a sparkling, social, and charismatic individual.

☽ in Cancer

You're warmhearted and generous to a fault. Your friends and loved ones are lucky to have you around.

☽ in Leo

My, what an extrovert you are! You were born to be on the big silver screen, and chances are you'll get there sooner rather than later.

☽ in Virgo
Not as dramatic as other Leos, nor as self-centered. With a Virgo moon, you're more restrained—and all the better for that.

☽ in Libra
Image is everything! How you look, how you perform, how others see you. And it works wonders.

☽ in Scorpio
You tend to brood over the tiniest slight. You need to ease up and go with the flow.

☽ in Sagittarius
What verve, what spirit, what élan! You're a true performer and no messing.

☽ in Capricorn
You're a born leader—inspired, enthusiastic, and far-sighted. You leave others in the shade.

☽ in Aquarius
Never lose faith in yourself—your far-out ideas could make you famous one day.

☽ in Pisces
Romance is a big thing in your life. If you go about it the right way, it could make you very successful one day.

compatibility

Who turns you on, Leo? Who makes your heart skip a beat? It has to be another fire sign. Sagittarians and Aries can match your ardor, keep the flame burning in your heart, and turn up the heat of passion beyond boiling point. They're the ones, too, who can give you the depth of love and commitment you're looking for in a romance. But air signs also know how to light your fire and how to maintain that element of fun and light-heartedness between you. When controlled, fire and water can produce steam. That's positive energy. All too often, though, water will douse the embers—an analogy that you can apply to relationships with any of the water signs. And members of the earth element can be too serious and stolid for you. Check out the Celestial Combinations, opposite, for a better picture of your perfect partner. And don't forget, you can use either your sun or moon sign to find that special combination.

LOVE HEART RATINGS

perilous = ❤

problematical = ❤❤

possible = ❤❤❤

promising = ❤❤❤❤

perfect = ❤❤❤❤❤

Celestial Combinations

YOUR SUN OR MOON SIGN WITH:

Aries   Big egos, big energy, big fire. Wonderful! ❤❤❤❤❤

Taurus   A gritty clash of stubborn temperaments. ❤❤

Gemini   Fun, glamour, champagne, pizzazz. Great. ❤❤❤❤

Cancer   Yes, if you're prepared to stay home nights. ❤❤❤

Leo   You're both superstars and super-everything. ❤❤❤❤❤

Virgo   Yikes! A conflict of hot emotion versus cold reason. ❤

Libra   A classy duo who appreciate the high life together. ❤❤❤❤

Scorpio   You're both so powerful—this could be a struggle. ❤❤

Sagittarius   Sexy, fiery, exciting—you're made for one another! ❤❤❤❤❤

Capricorn   Ouch! This one will cramp your style big time. ❤

Aquarius   Opposites can attract, and this one intrigues you. ❤❤❤

Pisces   You're two romantics but, alas, with different needs. ❤❤

Sensible

Intelligent

Organized

Honest

Practical

Altruistic

Logical

Virgo

Dates: August 24–September 23

Ruling Planet: Mercury

Element: Earth

Colors: Bottle green, blue, russet

Flowers: Anemone, buttercup

Precious Stone: Sardonyx

♍ Virgo

about you

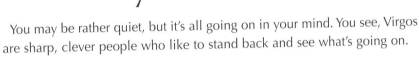

You may be rather quiet, but it's all going on in your mind. You see, Virgos are sharp, clever people who like to stand back and see what's going on.

Intelligent and observant, you can size up a situation at a glance. You're a genius at seeing through people and reading between the lines. No one has a better eye for detail or for perfection, either—although this means you can be over-critical, and too ready to pick holes in other people and situations.

Unlike the jazzier members of the Zodiac, you're restrained and demure. Bold and bright just isn't your thing—and you'd hate to be over-the-top.

You have a fantastic amount of common sense, a dry wit with a wicked talent for one-line put-downs, and you're brilliant at solving puzzles. No wonder, then, that your friends always come to you for advice.

But in matters of the heart, you can be shy. It's not that you're afraid of commitment, it's that you're afraid of being hurt. So you play a waiting game, getting to know someone slowly until you're sure you can trust them. That's why for Virgos love so often blossoms out of an existing friendship.

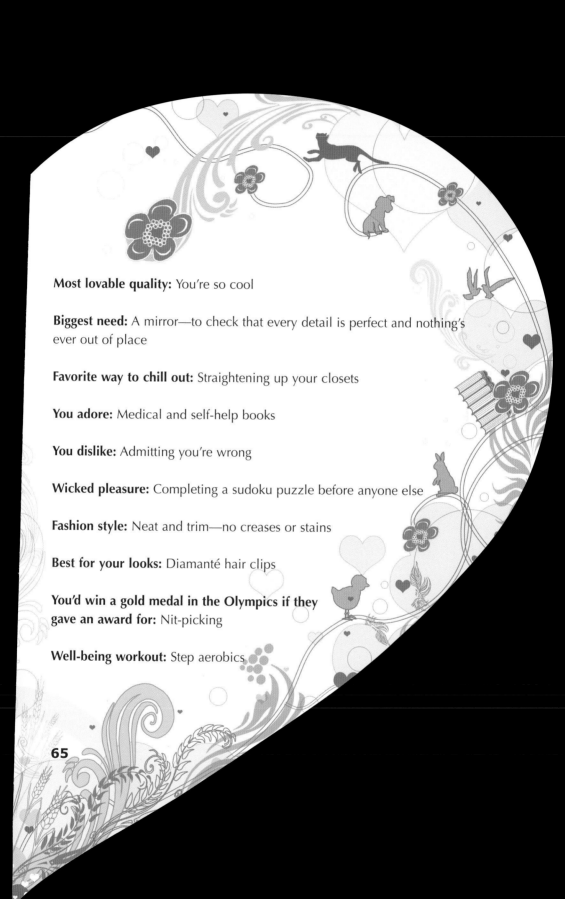

Most lovable quality: You're so cool

Biggest need: A mirror—to check that every detail is perfect and nothing's ever out of place

Favorite way to chill out: Straightening up your closets

You adore: Medical and self-help books

You dislike: Admitting you're wrong

Wicked pleasure: Completing a sudoku puzzle before anyone else

Fashion style: Neat and trim—no creases or stains

Best for your looks: Diamanté hair clips

You'd win a gold medal in the Olympics if they gave an award for: Nit-picking

Well-being workout: Step aerobics

65

heart & soul

Sugar-sweet goody-goody? Neat, tidy, orderly? Oh come on, there has to be more to you than that! And there is, if you add in your moon sign. Read on to discover more.

Incidentally, if you don't know your moon sign already, you can find instructions on how to calculate it on pages 15–19.

◑ in Aries

You're spirited and impulsive, which is great for making friends—and you're not shy in approaching someone you desire, either.

◑ in Taurus

This combination makes you rational and sensible, but also doubly earthy and doubly rooted.

◑ in Gemini

My, what a sharp tongue! And what a wicked sense of humor—just right for a stand-up comedian.

◑ in Cancer

Solid as a rock but prone to excess worry. What you need is to cultivate an attitude of "What will be, will be."

◑ in Leo

More outgoing than most Virgos, you have a love of pizzazz, which isn't half bad.

◐ in Virgo
With this moon, Virgo, you need to chill out more, which will help you to open up your heart and lift your game.

◐ in Libra
Your intelligence and charm are a formidable combination that will enable you to run rings around everyone else.

◐ in Scorpio
Cool and composed on the outside but with fire in your veins, you're an ice maiden with a passionate heart.

◐ in Sagittarius
Not only are you blessed with common sense, but you're wonderfully wise, too.

◐ in Capricorn
There's more to life than work, work, work, you know, Virgo—you need to lighten up!

◐ in Aquarius
Your idealistic heart brings out a strong community zeal and a desire to make the world a better place.

◐ in Pisces
Not only do you have the imagination, but you also have the technical skill. It's a winning formula.

compatibility

On a good day, you're discerning. At other times, you're selective. Usually, you're just downright fussy! It's all about perfection. Second best simply won't do, because a perfect partner has to be just that—perfect. So just what does constitute the perfect partner in your eyes? Well, someone who's intelligent, reliable, able to give you plenty of reassurance and boost your self-esteem. Other earth signs are on your wavelength. For example, Capricorn and Taurus are rock solid and always have something new to teach you, which, given your inquiring mind, is a delight. The water signs make sensitive partners; Cancer and Pisces especially think you're the bee's knees. Members of the fire and air groups, though, may sweep you off your feet; but actually you prefer to stay grounded. Anyway, check out the Celestial Combinations, opposite, to find where you make the best connections. And don't forget you can use both your sun and moon signs to find your ideal match.

LOVE HEART RATINGS

perilous =	❤
problematic =	❤❤
possible =	❤❤❤
promising =	❤❤❤❤
perfect =	❤❤❤❤❤

Celestial Combinations

YOUR SUN OR MOON SIGN WITH:

Aries	Best when you pursue your different interests.	❤❤
Taurus	Being so in tune is what makes this relationship so good.	❤❤❤❤❤❤
Gemini	An unusual friendship.	❤❤❤❤
Cancer	Strong bonds bind you together.	❤❤❤❤❤
Leo	This recipe requires a master class to make it succeed.	❤
Virgo	Work together and you could achieve big things!	❤❤❤❤❤❤
Libra	This partner is so undecided. Grrrr!	❤
Scorpio	Daring love.	❤❤❤
Sagittarius	You need to give each other space …	❤
Capricorn	You're so solid and together. Fantastic!	❤❤❤❤❤❤
Aquarius	It's challenging, but it will work if you're both bighearted.	❤❤
Pisces	You're both driven, but perhaps in different directions.	❤❤❤

Graceful

Romantic

Peace-loving

Social

Fair

Artistic

Poised

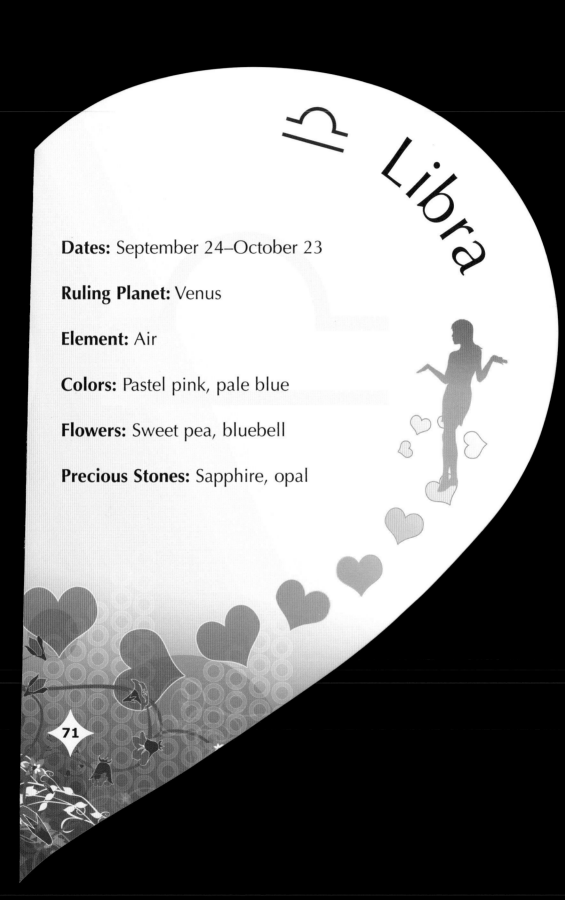

Libra ♎

Dates: September 24–October 23

Ruling Planet: Venus

Element: Air

Colors: Pastel pink, pale blue

Flowers: Sweet pea, bluebell

Precious Stones: Sapphire, opal

71

Libra

about you

Attractive, feminine, and graceful, as a Libran you do everything in style. You tend to have expensive tastes because image is so important to you. In fact, you probably have the best eye in town for designer labels. Whatever you buy, you usually go for quality rather than quantity.

Symbolically, Libra is represented by the scales; so for you, balance in life is essential. You like your environment to be lovely—with nothing gross or out of place. Nor do you like arguments or bad feelings. Falling out with people makes you physically ill, because it upsets your equilibrium. When it comes to your own problems and decisions, though, you can always see the other side of the argument and find it very difficult to make up your mind.

You're drawn to music, dance, and the arts. But diplomacy is your greatest skill—getting along with people, settling their differences, sorting out problems. It's your charm that wins people around.

In the Zodiac, Libra is the ruler of relationships. And because you're so pleasant and sociable, you make friends easily. You're a romantic through and through and never happier than when you're part of a twosome.

Most lovable quality: Making other people feel good about themselves

Biggest need: A soul mate

Favorite way to chill out: Giving yourself a makeover

You adore: Dating the coolest guy in town

You dislike: Mess—either of the physical or the emotional kind

Wicked pleasure: Buying the best designer outfit in the store

Fashion style: Elegant and well-groomed

Best for your looks: A great haircut

You'd win a gold medal in the Olympics if they gave an award for: The longest time it takes to get ready to go out

Well-being workout: Tennis

73

Libra

heart & soul

You've read what your sun sign says about you and your character, Libra. But your moon sign adds all the spicy bits. Curious? Read on. And if you don't know your moon sign already, you can find instructions on how to calculate it on pages 15–19.

◗ in Aries
You know your mind a good deal more than the average Libran, so you won't dither when you come across someone you really like.

◗ in Taurus
You're hugely talented, and as long as you enjoy your work, you're prepared to stick at it to ensure success.

◗ in Gemini
You have an excellent brain and are so persuasive. If you don't work in TV, you should go into the diplomatic corps.

◗ in Cancer
Sweet and caring, you work so much better and feel more comfortable when you have a close friend beside you.

◗ in Leo
There's something very beautiful and stylish about you. You have great taste and flair, too.

☽ in Virgo
Neat, tidy, and always precise, with your discerning eye the detail is everything.

☽ in Libra
You have good ideas and many talents, but your indecision holds you back. You must learn to strike while the iron is hot!

☽ in Scorpio
You're more decisive and tenacious than most Librans, which is good, and more intensely passionate, too.

☽ in Sagittarius
People you know really respect your judgment and come to you for advice – which you give brilliantly.

☽ in Capricorn
Because image and status are so important to you, only the very, very best will do.

☽ in Aquarius
Easygoing and amenable, you're very popular and attract loads of friends.

☽ in Pisces
You're not only dreamy because you're so creative, you're also dreamy because you're an absolutely desirable, dreamy chick!

compatibility

A guy would have to be really fit and gorgeous to even get a look-in where you're concerned. As you know, for Librans, appearances matter. Companionship is as important to you, too. After all, Libra is the sign of partners and partnerships, and you're never happier than when you're coupled up. But who is your dream-boat? Who takes your breath away, sets your heart a-flutter, and makes you feel like a star? A Leo can do all those things. So, too, can a Sagittarian. You and fire signs make a dream team. If you're looking for balance and harmony, you can find it within your own air element with a Gemini or an Aquarian and, of course, another Libran. But you may not feel quite so at ease with a partner belonging to the earth group, and you're probably out of your depth with the water signs. The Celestial Combinations, opposite, will tell you more. Check them out.

LOVE HEART RATINGS

perilous = ❤

problematical = ❤❤

possible = ❤❤❤

promising = ❤❤❤❤

perfect = ❤❤❤❤❤

Celestial Combinations

YOUR SUN OR MOON SIGN WITH:

Aries	A tantalizing attraction of opposites.	♥♥♥
Taurus	You're a charming couple in every way.	♥♥♥
Gemini	What an exquisite combination!	♥♥♥♥♥
Cancer	Be prepared to give up your freedom, OK?	♥
Leo	Plenty of mutual rapport and respect make this a winner.	♥♥♥♥
Virgo	If you need grounding, you'll find it here.	♥♥
Libra	So refined!	♥♥♥♥♥
Scorpio	You could be very good for each other if you try.	♥♥♥
Sagittarius	A very strong and auspicious match.	♥♥♥♥
Capricorn	You have to be mature to make this work.	♥
Aquarius	Oh, you think so alike!	♥♥♥♥♥
Pisces	Looking for affection? This partner has plenty to give.	♥♥♥

Magnetic

Mysterious

Deep

Intense

Passionate

Sultry

Sexy

78

♏ Scorpio

Dates: October 24–November 22

Ruling Planet: Pluto

Element: Water

Colors: Deep red, black

Flower: Amaryllis

Precious Stones: Garnet, opal, jasper

♏ Scorpio

about you

Wow! You're a fascinating creature—deep, powerful, and mysterious. In appearance, you're rather striking—sexy, curvaceous, and strong-featured, with a head of shiny, flowing hair. And that way you have of standing aloof and wearing dark colors conjures up an air of essential mystique.

You're a true individual, someone who likes to do your own thing and never be a fashion victim. You love to look sexy and to stand out from the crowd. If the truth were told, you're a bit of a rebel.

Intuition is one of your greatest assets. You possess an uncanny ability to pick up on what others are thinking. You're persistent and determined, and once you get your teeth into a plan or project, you hang in there right to the bitter end.

Because you read people so well, you can sometimes be manipulative. In relationships, you're loyal and true— qualities that you expect in both friends and partners. But if someone hurts you, you *will* get even—no matter how long it takes. Then out comes that famous poisonous sting in the scorpion's tail! A Scorpio never forgives or forgets.

Most lovable quality: You're so mysterious

Biggest need: Privacy

Favorite way to chill out: Reading a thriller

You adore: Being in total control

You dislike: Being crossed

Wicked pleasure: Knowing that people admire you

Fashion style: Sexy, sultry, naughty

Best for your looks: Dark glasses

You'd win a gold medal in the Olympics if they gave an award for: Jealousy

Well-being workout: Kick boxing

heart & soul

Your sun sign description is pretty intense stuff, don't you think, Scorpio? But will your moon sign arouse your passion or fire your longing? Read on if your want to know more.

However, if you don't know your moon sign already, you can find instructions on how to calculate it on pages 15–19.

◑ in Aries
Hugely passionate, deep and intense, you can be pretty unstoppable when you want something—or someone!

◑ in Taurus
You're a powerful individual with a strong, stubborn streak that ensures you reach your goal come what may.

◑ in Gemini
Cool customer! You're a fascinating and interesting mixture. You're clever and have a terrific imagination.

◑ in Cancer
You're more tender-hearted than the average Scorpio, and you love looking after people.

◑ in Leo
Strong and determined, but also emotionally changeable—your unpredictability makes you interesting.

☽ in Virgo
You're a caring person with masses of integrity and a fascination for medical matters.

☽ in Libra
You're oh so sophisticated—cool on the surface but emotionally deep. You positively ooze sex appeal.

☽ in Scorpio
You have a labyrinth of hidden depths. When you set your heart on something, you won't stop until you get it!

☽ in Sagittarius
You have a wonderfully investigative curiosity and would do well in the legal profession.

☽ in Capricorn
This moon stabilizes your emotions and helps you to focus. It gives you huge drive and immense willpower, too.

☽ in Aquarius
Your strength lies in figuring out people and situations and in being able to read between the lines so clearly.

☽ in Pisces
Because you're always analyzing people and their behavior, you'd make a terrific psychologist one day.

Scorpio

compatibility

Who lights your fire, Scorpio? Who is the challenge you can't resist? Try a water sign. Somehow, they seem to know where to find the key to your heart. Perhaps it's because no one understands your needs better than a Pisces, a Cancerian, and, of course, another Scorpio. But you can make equally sweet music with the earth signs. For a start, you know that you can trust a Virgo—and for you trust is an essential ingredient in your relationships. Capricorn, too, makes a staunch and steady soul mate, which is good because you like to know where you stand with a partner. That's why you find members of the air signs a bit perplexing—they're all over the place. And it's the same with the fire bunch: exciting at first but quite exhausting in the long term. To know more, all you have to do is check out the Celestial Combinations, opposite. Match up either your sun or moon sign to find your perfect mate.

LOVE HEART RATINGS

perilous = ❤

problematical = ❤❤

possible = ❤❤❤

promising = ❤❤❤❤

perfect = ❤❤❤❤❤

Celestial Combinations

YOUR SUN OR MOON SIGN WITH:

Aries	A rollercoaster of a relationship.	❤❤❤❤
Taurus	Strong, stubborn twosome, but quite romantic.	❤❤❤
Gemini	Uh-oh. On different wavelengths.	❤
Cancer	Irresistible magnetism!	❤❤❤❤❤
Leo	Sharing power is the secret to success here.	❤❤❤
Virgo	You're both far too intense and need to ease up.	❤❤❤
Libra	Making concessions will help this love to survive.	❤❤
Scorpio	An alluring fascination.	❤❤❤❤❤
Sagittarius	You're worlds apart but love could draw you closer.	❤❤
Capricorn	Terrific attraction.	❤❤❤❤
Aquarius	Ooops. Neither wants to give in to the other.	❤❤❤
Pisces	A stunningly successful relationship. Bravo!	❤❤❤❤❤

Open

Friendly

Enthusiastic

Philosophical

Warm

Noisy

Lucky

86

Dates: November 23–December 21

Ruling Planet: Jupiter

Element: Fire

Colors: Purple, violet, indigo

Flowers: Narcissus, pink

Precious Stones: Turquoise, topaz

Sagittarius

Sagittarius ↑

↑ about you

The nicest thing about Sagittarians is their friendly manner. You positively radiate warmth, and that ready smile is guaranteed to draw people. You're such a lively, happy soul that you brighten up the room just by being there.

You're also one of the most easygoing people on the planet. You breeze through life with a happy-go-lucky attitude and an expectation that everything will turn out right in the end—and what's more it usually does! But then, Sagittarius is the luckiest sign in the Zodiac.

Not only that, but you're so intuitive, too. Often you say something and it hits the bull's-eye. Mind you, the truth can hurt, so it would pay to be a little more tactful, especially when around sensitive souls.

You're definitely not patient when it comes to details, because as a Sagittarian you prefer the bigger picture. That's why you like travel, foreign languages, and faraway places so much—your love of freedom impels you to gallop off in search of new adventures. You're a great friend, but you shy away from committing yourself to a one-to-one. Perhaps because you always think the grass may be greener over the next horizon.

Most lovable quality: Your cheerfulness

Biggest need: Space

Favorite way to chill out: Getting in the car and just *going* …

You adore: Change, adventure, a new challenge

You dislike: Being told that something simply isn't possible

Wicked pleasure: Visiting a garage sale and finding a first edition of *Bridget Jones's Diary*

Fashion style: Comfortable, loose, sporty

Best for your looks: Great running shoes

You'd win a gold medal in the Olympics if they gave an award for: Making a gaffe

Well-being workout: Horse-riding

heart & soul

Are you really quite as restless as your sun sign suggests?

Perhaps your moon sign will give a more balanced picture of the real you, so check it out here.

Incidentally, if you don't know your moon sign already, you can find instructions on how to calculate it on pages 15–19.

☽ in Aries

Sociable, gregarious, and romantic, you're great fun to be with and tend to be attracted to adventurous people.

☽ in Taurus

Steady and sober, you're kind and helpful and take your responsibilities very seriously.

☽ in Gemini

Ants in your pants, Saggie? You're certainly adventurous, and you tend to take on whatever grabs your imagination.

☽ in Cancer

Do you roam or stay home? That's the dilemma this moon poses. A bit of both is the ideal solution.

☽ in Leo

You're a hugely popular, charismatic person and a bundle of laughs (but sometimes a little o.t.t.). Want to be in showbiz? Perfect!

90

☾ in Virgo

Wise and thoughtful, but also essentially kind, you're always ready to help those in need.

☾ in Libra

You're a "people person," and you'll always have lots of friends scattered all over the world.

☾ in Scorpio

You're always probing, testing, investigating, and asking questions—you've just got that kind of curious nature.

☾ in Sagittarius

Have you got itchy feet, or what? You're restless and want to experience everything the world has to offer.

☾ in Capricorn

Although you're ambitious, you have a charitable nature, and you want to do good in the world.

☾ in Aquarius

You're sharp, clever, on your toes, inspired, and quite unique. In fact, you're extraordinary!

☾ in Pisces

You're truly farsighted and should trust your inner voice—it could make you a fortune one day!

compatibility

You may be sporty and outgoing, but you're quite a wise philosopher in your own way. So your soul mate needs to be someone who can match both your love of living life to the full and your interest in the deeper meaning of life. An Aquarian would fill that bill nicely. In fact, fire and air go together well. Members of both these elements are lively and chatty, and they're physically and mentally stimulating, too. Moreover, since you're such an independent creature, air signs will suit you because they're able to give you all the space you need. But as a Sagittarian, you're also passionate and romantic. If you want a hot match, you need look no further than a Leo or an Aries. Be wary of water, and go easy on earth, for these are the signs that will try to tie you down. Want to know more? Study the Celestial Combinations, opposite. You can match either your sun or moon sign to get the right result.

LOVE HEART RATINGS

perilous = ❤

problematical = ❤❤

possible = ❤❤❤

promising = ❤❤❤❤

perfect = ❤❤❤❤❤

Celestial Combinations

YOUR SUN OR MOON SIGN WITH:

Aries   An exciting combination—never a dull moment!   ♥♥♥♥♥

Taurus   Respect will keep this friendship going.   ♥

Gemini   You may be opposites, but you're so invigorating.   ♥♥♥

Cancer   You'll need to watch what you say—Cancerians are sensitive!   ♥♥

Leo   Little beats this love story. It's passionate and strong.   ♥♥♥♥♥♥

Virgo   Only if you find a way to unite your differing goals.   ♥

Libra   You're so good for each other!   ♥♥♥♥

Scorpio   You'll need to work harder to find magic here.   ♥♥

Sagittarius What a wonderful hunger for life you both share!   ♥♥♥♥♥

Capricorn   Encourage each other's best qualities to make this work.   ♥

Aquarius   A terrific fun-loving and outward-looking pair.   ♥♥♥♥

Pisces   Okay, as long as you both share the same dream.   ♥♥

Ambitious

Industrious

Determined

Shy

Loyal

Mature

Authoritative

94

♑ Capricorn

Date: December 22–January 20

Ruling Planet: Saturn

Element: Earth

Colors: Navy blue, indigo, medium green

Flower: Pansy

Precious Stone: Onyx

Capricorn

about you

You're a cool chick, Capricorn, and being an earth sign, you're sensible, mature, and realistic, too. You know that if you want to get anywhere you have to work hard. And since you're ambitious and determined to succeed, you're happy to roll up your sleeves and put in long hours of hard work.

There's something special about you, Capricorn. You're born with an old head on young shoulders; and because of that, you take a serious attitude to life—which is just as well, for you often have a lot of responsibility to cope with.

Fashion-wise, you look great and feel comfortable in smart, classically styled clothes. You go for dark colors and good quality. And since you're status-conscious, you love designer labels.

Because of your serious nature, people who don't know you well can fail to realize how warmhearted you are. Add to that your caution in getting to know people, and you see why it can take you time to make friends. With romance, you need to let others discover your special qualities. And when they do, they appreciate what a trustworthy, loyal person you are, capable of giving true, deep, genuine, and lasting affection.

Most lovable quality: Your dry wit

Biggest need: To keep busy

Favorite way to chill out: Writing lists, making plans, setting agendas

You adore: Only the best

You dislike: Someone else taking charge

Wicked pleasure: Swanking about in your latest designer purchase

Fashion style: A fairly formal, tailored look

Best for your looks: Smart trousers

You'd win a gold medal in the Olympics if they gave an award for: Snobbishness

Well-being workout: Line dancing

heart & soul

It would be a funny old world if all you Capricorns were identical, wouldn't it? So what makes you special, different, and unique? It's the way your sun sign combines with your moon sign. Skeptical? Read on.

And if you don't know your moon sign already, you can find instructions on how to calculate it on pages 15–19.

☽ in Aries

No room for gloomy moods with this moon, which lifts your spirits and gives you va va voom!

☽ in Taurus

You're a totally together chick who knows value when she sees it and who adores all the creature comforts that money can buy.

☽ in Gemini

Highly intelligent and analytical, you have a great flair for organization —and a dry wit, too.

☽ in Cancer

So responsible, especially toward those you love, you're also emotionally tender and should try to stop worrying.

☽ in Leo

You have an eye for expensive goods, and you like to have your designer labels on display for all to see.

☽ in Virgo
Perhaps one of the hardest-working people in the Zodiac, you like to follow the rules and do things right.

☽ in Libra
With that discerning eye for beauty, you're prepared to work hard so that you can afford nice things.

☽ in Scorpio
Single-minded and choosy about your friends, you're very selective about whom you hang out with.

☽ in Sagittarius
You may work hard, but the good thing is that you certainly know when to stop and enjoy yourself, too.

☽ in Capricorn
True, you're serious, but you also know how to let off steam for the occasional crazy five minutes.

☽ in Aquarius
Your key to fame and fortune is to leave yesterday behind and focus on tomorrow.

☽ in Pisces
You have a terrific imagination, which makes your life loads of fun!

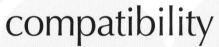

Capricorn

compatibility

You're definitely down-to-earth, Capricorn, and are drawn to people who are equally grounded and mature. So it's no surprise that you make a beeline for Taurus and Virgo, because, like you, they belong to the earth element. You take relationships very seriously, and so do they. Taurus, especially, will put you at ease and show you what you're missing out on. Members of the water signs also resonate nicely with you and bring some intoxicating passion to the mix. A love match with either Scorpio or Cancer, for example, is a potent brew. You may find the air group too volatile, as a whole. Geminis are clever, but you think them superficial; Libra shilly-shally too much, and you can take or leave Aquarians. The same applies to the fire signs, to whom you may want to give a wide berth. Find out from the Celestial Combinations, opposite, who would make your ideal match. Don't forget, you can use both your sun and moon signs to make your best selection.

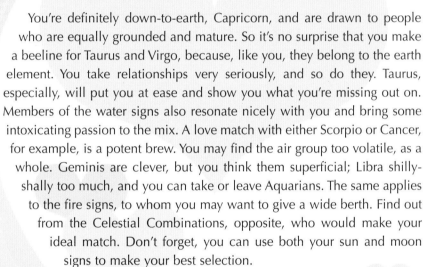

LOVE HEART RATINGS

perilous = ❤

problematical = ❤❤

possible = ❤❤❤

promising = ❤❤❤❤

perfect = ❤❤❤❤❤

100

Celestial Combinations

YOUR SUN OR MOON SIGN WITH:

Aries	Friends, perhaps, but alas, not much more.	♥♥♥
Taurus	A bright pairing with a bright future.	♥♥♥♥♥
Gemini	You agree to disagree in order to find harmony.	♥
Cancer	This relationship may stretch you too far.	♥♥♥
Leo	You make an ambitious team.	♥♥♥
Virgo	Solid, sensible, and well-matched pair.	♥♥♥♥♥
Libra	You're different types, but you complement each other.	♥
Scorpio	Fabulous! You hit it off from the word go.	♥♥♥♥
Sagittarius	You'll get along only if you both try really hard.	♥
Capricorn	Great! But life shouldn't be all work and no play.	♥♥♥♥♥
Aquarius	You'll find strength and stability here.	♥♥♥
Pisces	You may prefer someone more robust.	♥♥♥

Independent

Eccentric

Farsighted

Innovative

Inquisitive

Humanitarian

Avant-garde

102

Aquarius

Dates: January 21–February 19

Ruling Planet: Uranus

Element: Air

Color: Electric blue

Flower: Snowdrop

Precious Stone: Amethyst

Aquarius

about you

Aquarians are natural beauties; so you're probably blessed with a fine bone structure and deep, attractive eyes. Although you like to be fashionably up-to-date, you often add quirky items that make you stand out.

Of all the signs, this is the one that's described as the most futuristic. An ingenious imagination, an inquiring mind, and an advanced way of thinking all combine to give you an edge that's quite groundbreaking. Being so inventive gives you a flair for the new and the unusual. You're an innovator, forever trying to improve the things we use and the way we live.

Because you're such a progressive thinker, there's not much about people's behavior that fazes you. You're a tolerant live-and-let-live sort of person, and it's precisely this openness and acceptance of others that wins you so many friends. Sociable and popular, you're a great team player, who finds it easy to fit into any environment or group gathering.

But on a personal level you tend to hide your feelings, preferring to come across as cool or distant. For you, friendship in a relationship is almost more important than romance.

Most lovable quality: Always being up for something new

Biggest need: To be part of the latest craze

Favorite way to chill out: Hanging out with your friends

You adore: Trendy gadgets

You dislike: The same old, same old …

Wicked pleasure: Hunting through a junk shop to turn up a treasure

Fashion style: Ultra-modern with an offbeat twist

Best for your looks: Jeans with a tuxedo

You'd win a gold medal in the Olympics if they gave an award for: Inventing the weirdest thing that will catch on in five years' time

Well-being workout: T'ai chi

105

heart & soul

Being the clever Aquarian that you are means that you probably know a thing or two about astrology already. So chances are you're aware that your sun sign is modified by your moon sign. Read on to find out how. Incidentally, if you don't know your moon sign already, you can find instructions on how to calculate it on pages 15–19.

☽ in Aries
Bright and charismatic, you're a girl with a mission. You won't ever be short of followers or admirers.

☽ in Taurus
You may not want to admit this openly, but you're actually very protective of the things—and people—you love.

☽ in Gemini
You're a real whizz kid, kiddo! You've got electricity, you've got vision, you've got what it takes.

☽ in Cancer
You know what? Despite your breezy Aquarian manner, you're really quite a softy underneath.

☽ in Leo
Lights, music, action! Dramatic, colorful, and flamboyant, you'll probably win an Oscar one day.

☽ in Virgo
You're super-intelligent, and if *you* don't understand what rocket science is all about, who does?

☽ in Libra
Everybody wants to be your friend, which isn't at all surprising, as you're such fascinating company to be with.

☽ in Scorpio
If you let it, your heart will rule your head, which can feel a little strange for someone as streetwise as you.

☽ in Sagittarius
Because you're one of life's true adventurers and pioneers, you should never be afraid to try something new.

☽ in Capricorn
You don't want to rock the boat, but if you think something is unfair, you'll want to do something to make it right.

☽ in Aquarius
You know what gives you a great buzz, Aquarius? Anything offbeat. You're different—and enjoy being that way.

☽ in Pisces
You're an interesting mix of deep and determined, passionate and persistent, sultry and sexy. Phew!

Aquarius

compatibility

What you don't want in a relationship is a clingy partner. You see, although you yearn to be part of a couple, you also value your independence. So your ideal mate will be someone who knows precisely when you need a cuddle and when you need to have your own space. Tough call? Not at all! There's Sagittarius for a start. And Aries. Both belong to the fire signs, and as we know, fire and air are fabulously combustible. These two will light a fire that will blaze in your heart. The other air signs —Gemini and Libra—are equally compatible with you. Both are sociable and outgoing, so there's plenty here to keep you amused and entertained. You probably have less in common with the earth and water signs, unless your Moon sign belongs to either of these elements. Take a look at the Celestial Combinations, opposite. Match up either your sun or your moon sign to find your perfect pairing.

LOVE HEART RATINGS
perilous = ♥
problematical = ♥♥
possible = ♥♥♥
promising = ♥♥♥♥
perfect = ♥♥♥♥♥

Celestial Combinations

YOUR SUN OR MOON SIGN WITH:

Aries   Exhilarating—but sometimes exhausting, too.   ❤❤❤

Taurus   A charming camaraderie, but you'll need to stay focused.   ❤

Gemini   Your relationship is wacky, wicked, and wonderful!

❤❤❤❤❤

Cancer   This romantic spark takes a long time to ignite.   ❤

Leo   This combination makes for glorious fireworks!   ❤❤❤

Virgo   A love of good works unites you.   ❤❤

Libra   Masses of mutual appreciation.   ❤❤❤❤❤

Scorpio   Curiosity keeps you interested in each other.   ❤❤❤

Sagittarius You're both unconventional, but you're so in synch.

❤❤❤❤

Capricorn   Ouch! There are power conflicts here.   ❤❤

Aquarius   Shared experiences and a meeting of minds.

❤❤❤❤❤

Pisces   A surprisingly stimulating rapport.

❤❤❤

Sensitive

Idealistic

Sympathetic

Considerate

Impressionable

Clairvoyant

Dreamy

Pisces

Dates: February 20–March 20

Ruling Planet: Neptune

Element: Water

Color: Blue-green

Flowers: Lilac, iris

Precious Stone: Aquamarine

Pisces

♓ about you

It's that soft, faraway look in your eyes that instantly gives you away as a Piscean. And like other members of your sign, your eyes (which may be gray-green in color) tend to turn down sleepily at the corners.

Pisceans are dreamy people who live with their heads in the clouds. How often do you fantasize or get lost in reveries? If you're typical of your sign, the answer will be: all too often. You're so creative, too. You can make up wonderful stories, write tender poems, compose beautiful tunes, and paint lovely pictures. No wonder you're drawn to literature, art, and music.

Because many Pisceans are also psychic, you're probably highly receptive to the vibes around you. This gives you the amazing ability to tune in to other people's feelings. It's this sensitivity that makes you such a compassionate and warmhearted person. And it's your gentleness and vulnerability that make you so loved.

When it comes to matters of the heart, you are the ultimate romantic! You're a fairytale princess, who's looking for your knight in shining armor, for a cottage with roses around the door, and, of course, for a happy-ever-after ending.

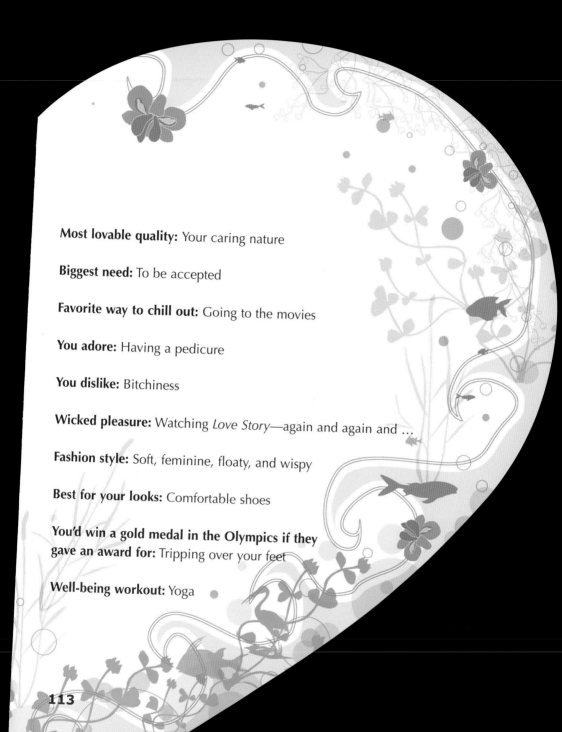

Most lovable quality: Your caring nature

Biggest need: To be accepted

Favorite way to chill out: Going to the movies

You adore: Having a pedicure

You dislike: Bitchiness

Wicked pleasure: Watching *Love Story*—again and again and ...

Fashion style: Soft, feminine, floaty, and wispy

Best for your looks: Comfortable shoes

You'd win a gold medal in the Olympics if they gave an award for: Tripping over your feet

Well-being workout: Yoga

113

Pisces

heart & soul

There's more to you than just a fishy tale, Pisces. Because, as you well know, people are made up of lots of different facets. It's the moon that puts a spin on your personality, and if you want to know how, read on.

By the way, if you don't know your moon sign already, you can find instructions on how to calculate it on pages 15–19.

◗ in Aries

You may be shy on the surface, but emotionally your feelings are as tough as steel. You know what you want and how to get it.

◗ in Taurus

This moon keeps your feet on the ground and your head in your books. Terrific!

◗ in Gemini

You could be the next J.K. Rowling, so keep writing!

◗ in Cancer

You must admit that your crab shell can be great protection when you need a little shelter for your tender heart.

◗ in Leo

Those dreams about romance and fantasies about a life of luxury aren't all just pie in the sky, Pisces—you can make them happen.

☽ in Virgo

Have you got X-ray eyes or something? Being as perceptive as you are means you can read a person like a book.

☽ in Libra

You tend to look at the world through rose-colored glasses, don't you Pisces? The time has come to ditch them and get real!

☽ in Scorpio

You're a bona fide water babe—super-slinky and devastatingly gorgeous, too.

☽ in Sagittarius

If you ever doubt yourself, just remember that Einstein was a Pisces—and guess what? His moon was in Sagittarius, too!

☽ in Capricorn

You really don't need to be quite so bashful, you know. Believe in yourself, and the world will believe in you.

☽ in Aquarius

Born with this combination means that no way will you let the grass grow under your feet.

☽ in Pisces

You're in a class of your own. You're a dear, sweet soul, and after they made you, they broke the mold.

Pisces

compatibility

Being in love—and being loved back—is your ultimate dream. This is what you long for, and when you find your caring, sensitive soul mate, you're in seventh heaven. Of course, belonging to the water element means that you get on well with the other signs in your own group. Cancerians and Scorpios are certainly on your emotional wavelength. But what many Pisceans need is stability and strength, qualities that you'll find in abundance among the earth signs. For example, Taurus will anchor you while at the same time share your love of creativity, music, and art. You can melt into the arms of your Virgo or Capricorn hero and know you are safe. On the other hand, a guy belonging to the fire signs may seem dashing and romantic, but his lack of sensitivity will eventually disappoint you. The same goes for the air signs. Match your sun or moon sign in Celestial Combinations, opposite, to discover where your love destiny lies.

LOVE HEART RATINGS

perilous = ❤

problematical = ❤❤

possible = ❤❤❤

promising = ❤❤❤❤

perfect = ❤❤❤❤❤

Celestial Combinations

YOUR SUN OR MOON SIGN WITH:

Aries	Balancing freedom and possessiveness is paramount.	❤❤
Taurus	This team's got a lot going for it.	❤❤❤
Gemini	A delicate and fragile romance.	❤❤
Cancer	Twin souls traveling the same path.	❤❤❤❤❤
Leo	A supportive union if you each give it time.	❤❤
Virgo	The key is learning to compromise.	❤❤❤
Libra	A beautiful friendship.	❤❤❤
Scorpio	A primitive magnetism pulls you together.	❤❤❤❤❤
Sagittarius	Your shared philosophy of life makes you a viable team.	❤
Capricorn	You're really good for each other.	❤❤❤❤
Aquarius	A couple of free spirits who'll get along just fine.	❤❤❤
Pisces	On cloud nine.	❤❤❤❤❤

117

The stars may choose when you meet your **soul mate**, but there's a lot you can do to help destiny along …

when to meet
& when to
move on

time for living & loving

You can use the Moon Charts on pages 16–19 to find out which sign the moon is in on any particular day. All you have to do is follow the instructions; but instead of starting with your date of birth, work from the date of the day you wish to find out about. When you know the sign, just look it up below and tune in to that day's special vibes.

When the moon is in Aries events happen quickly. Wear red to attract admiring glances. A relationship started now will be thrilling but short-lived.

When the moon is in Taurus it's a sensual day. Wear light blue to impress. Meeting someone new today could be the start of a lovely, long romance.

When the moon is in Gemini it's a day full of news—people talk a lot, the phone rings, and invitations drop through the mail slot. A romantic encounter started today will be a gas.

When the moon is in Cancer home is where the heart is. If you are seeking a long and beautiful friendship, look for your soul mate today.

When the moon is in Leo—oh, the drama! Wear orange. Whoever you meet for the first time today will spoil you rotten and treat you like a queen.

120

When the moon is in Virgo people are clear-sighted. Think green. Hooking up with someone new? This relationship will be more talk than walk.

When the moon is in Libra it's great for romantic dates. Think beauty, elegance, and refinement. Pastel shades are winners today.

When the moon is in Scorpio it's a secretive sort of day. Gossip and scandal do the rounds. Meeting someone new? Be sure you know what you're getting yourself into …

When the moon is in Sagittarius people are curious and restless. New love today will be enlightening, but lovers may be soon parted.

When the moon is in Capricorn don't bend the rules or you'll pay the price. A relationship that starts today will endure.

When the moon is in Aquarius friendship is key, so socialize. Although electricity drives a relationship that sparks today, it may fizzle out just as quickly.

When the moon is in Pisces imaginative ideas are flowing. Greenish blue is today's color. People are impressionable and fall in love or develop crushes easily.

hot dates

What makes you happy? What pushes all your buttons, excites you, and unlocks your passion? Consult your love sign below for the answers—and leave your book open on this page for your man to read!

Aries You love action, excitement, and speed, so any kind of sporting sensation—whether you're just watching or taking part together—hits the bull's-eye. Going to a thrills-and-spills movie on your date, to an amusement park, or spending the day at the fair will give you that rush of adrenaline that makes this a lover's tryst to remember.

Taurus Because you're a terrific dancer and you love music, being taken to a club or a concert is a surefire winner for a Taurean like you. You love the sensation of touch, so make sure you dance close and tight. Or else spend a pleasant Saturday afternoon mooching around the shops together, and then drop in to watch the latest romantic movie at your nearest multiplex.

Gemini It's got to be a party, where you can flirt with your guy like mad and keep him (and everyone else) amused with your sparkling wit. Or sit in a coffee bar and just talk together about your feelings, your interests, your friends. It's intimate tête-à-têtes like these that draw you closer to the one you love.

122

Cancer You're a romantic who just loves surprises—like an unexpected gift that comes beautifully wrapped. It doesn't have to be expensive, because for you, it's definitely the thought that counts. You're drawn to water, too, so a stroll along a river, or a day at the beach would make you happy.

Leo You have expensive tastes, adore being spoiled, and love going into swish and swanky places. On a date, you want to be made to feel like a million dollars; and you are in your element when your admirer makes a big fuss of you. It doesn't matter what you do or where you go, as long as you're the center of his attention.

Virgo You're a true Nature's child and love simple things, such as a walk in the park or a picnic in the countryside. An evening mixing music together, studying, or playing intellectual games is so stimulating. Best of all, as you're amazingly tactile, is cozying up to your man on a garden bench as you chat and gaze up at the stars in the ink-black sky.

Libra Just being in love and part of a twosome with a really fit guy is sheer bliss for you. Physically being together, walking side by side, going to a movie, listening to music, playing a game of tennis—anything, as long as you're together—is what makes your heart skip a beat and puts you in your element on your dream date.

Scorpio Sitting close, holding hands, gazing deeply, deeply into each others' eyes pushes all the right buttons where a Scorpio is concerned. You're a passionate creature who craves intimacy and likes to get physical. A dark, quiet corner or the back seats at the movies when the lights go down is a date made in heaven for you.

Sagittarius Fun, fun, fun—that's what you want on your special date. To be comfortable and entertained without fuss and formality is essential. You're competitive and like to be "one of the guys," so bowling, for example, would be ideal. But you love to laugh, and a man who knows how to tickle you in the ribs will put stars in your eyes.

Capricorn You probably go for older guys who're serious, experienced, and well-off. What you're looking for in a date is someone formal who will take charge and won't rush you. You'll adore being whisked away to see a rock band playing, or while away an afternoon together in a music store or even go arm in arm on a cross-country hike.

Aquarius Your favorite date? Something spontaneous like an impromptu midnight swim. You like to be surprised, called on the phone, texted, emailed, or asked out when you least expect it. You're interested in people, so a party is a sure thing. But you'll also enjoy a virtual date, when you and your heartthrob can spend an evening flirting with each other online.

Pisces You're never happier than when in the arms of your latest squeeze. You're an incurable romantic, looking for a dreamy date straight out of a fairy tale—soft lights, gentle music, and whispered words of love. You don't have to go far; cuddling up with your hero on the sofa to watch a weepie is all it takes to put you in seventh heaven.

moving on

Until you find your Mr. Right, making and breaking relationships is all part of life's rich tapestry. Meeting and falling in love is the thrilling part. The difficult part is breaking up, because inevitably someone is going to get emotionally bruised. However, astrology has a few tricks up its sleeve, and if you follow the rules of cosmic timing, you can minimize the hurt, hassle, and heartache that splitting up can cause.

How to ditch an Aries: Go all weak and pathetic. Become a couch potato, and whine and snivel a lot every time he takes you out.

How to ditch a Taurus: Borrow his favorite DVD and, um, accidentally leave it on the bus. Develop very expensive tastes, and get him to spend loads of his money on you.

How to ditch a Gemini: Yawn every time he tells you a funny joke. Say you don't like going out any more, and nag him to stay in with you —become really, really boring.

How to ditch a Cancerian: Insist you go out more, and drag him to parties, to the stores, and to your friends' houses. Mess up his CD collection, and subtly criticize his mom's cooking.

How to ditch a Leo: Constantly look at yourself in the mirror, and talk about only you, you, you. Show him up in front of his pals.

126

How to ditch a Virgo: Cultivate disgusting habits, such as eating garlic and onions just before you kiss. Keep him waiting for at least half an hour every time you arrange to meet.

How to ditch a Libran: Dress like a bag lady. Be loud and embarrass him when you're out with his friends. Point out anything cheap and ugly, and say how much you adore it.

How to ditch a Scorpio: Become a rampant feminist. Stop being affectionate, and show you're losing interest in getting intimate with him. Obey all rules and regulations, and insist that he do so, too.

How to ditch a Sagittarian: Chatter on about the silliest, most trivial and inane things you can think of. Become really clingy. Text him all the time when he's out with his pals.

How to ditch a Capricorn: Spill makeup over his expensive jeans. Feign dislike for any gift he gives you. Go out looking crumpled and disheveled—especially when meeting his parents!

How to ditch an Aquarian: Fly into a jealous rage if he even glances at another girl. Be all over him like a rash. Insist he tell you in detail where he's been and what he's done when he's not with you.

How to ditch a Piscean: Pick fights over silly things. Show him you no longer share his taste in music, art, film, or fashion. Make really trivial excuses why you can't go out with him.

author's acknowledgments

I would like to thank everyone involved in *Love Signs* for making it such a gorgeous book: Grace Cheetham for coming up with this delightful concept, Ingrid Court-Jones for her skillful editing, Flatliner V2 for the wonderful illustrations, and Manisha Patel and Luana Gobbo for their sensitive, artistic eye—*un grosso abbraccio*. And, of course, DBP for making it all possible. It's been a fabulous team to work with.

publisher's notes

Neither the publishers nor the author can be held responsible for any foolish acts committed by readers who have found true love through this book. Because, as we all know, falling in love makes us do some silly things! However, both the publishers and the author would be happy to be invited to any weddings or christenings that may occur as a result of reading *Love Signs*.

For further information about the illustrator, please visit:
www.flatliner-v2.com

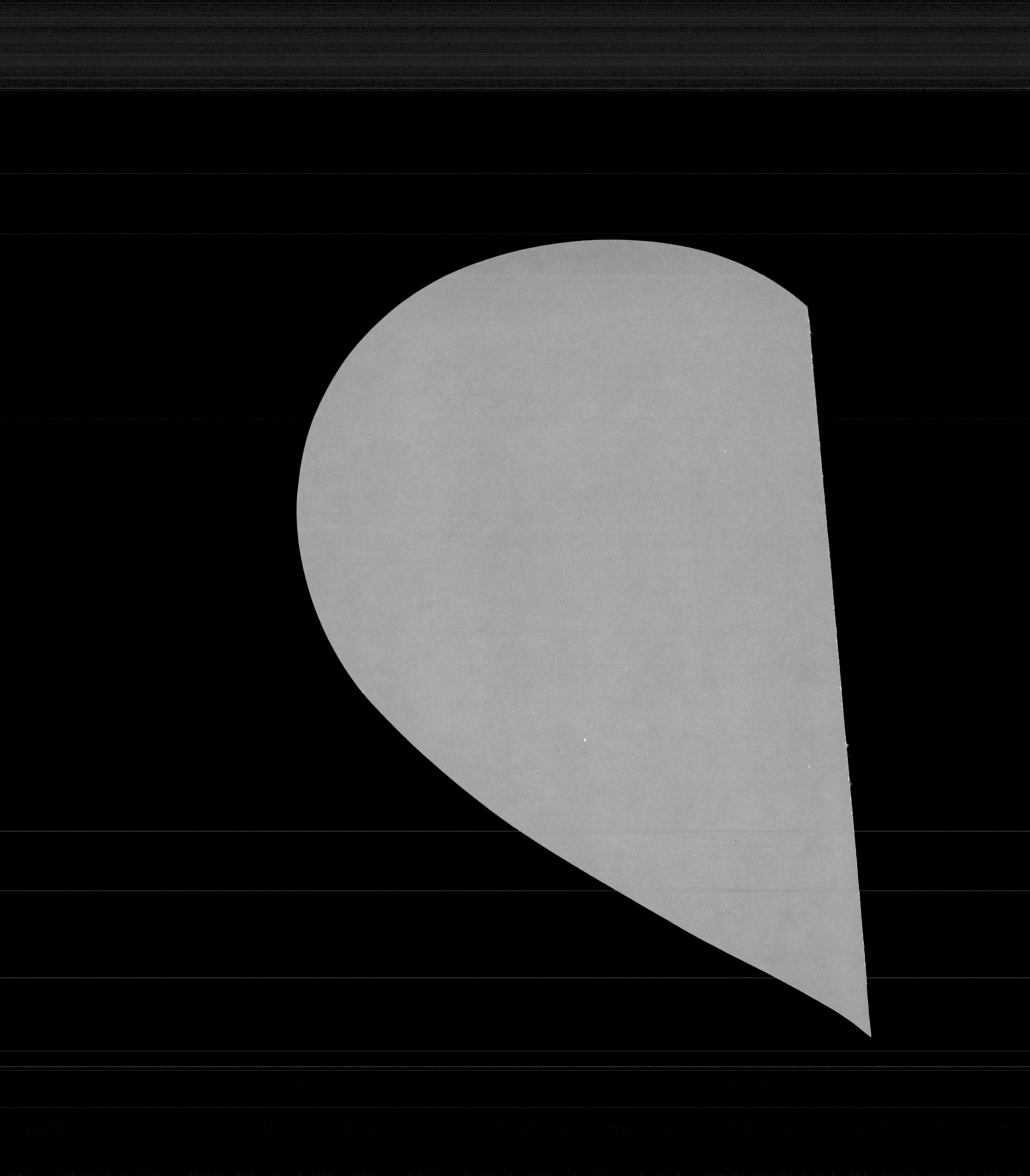